UN**BELIEVABLE!**

34 AMAZING FACTS ABOUT FOOTBALL

Matt Doeden

Lerner Publications ◆ Minneapolis

Lerner Publications Company
An imprint of Lerner Publishing Group, Inc.
241 First Avenue North
Minneapolis, MN 55401 USA

For reading levels and more information, look up this title at www.lernerbooks.com.

Main body text set in ITC Franklin Gothic Std.
Typeface provided by Adobe Systems.

Editor: Annie Zheng **Designer:** Mary Ross
Lerner team: Sue Marquis

Library of Congress Cataloging-in-Publication Data

Names: Doeden, Matt author.
Title: 34 amazing facts about football / Matt Doeden.
Other titles: Thirty-four amazing facts about football.
Description: Minneapolis, MN : Lerner Publications, [2024] | Series: UpDog books. Unbelievable! | Includes bibliographical references and index. | Audience: Ages 8–11 | Audience: Grades 2–3 | Summary: "Football is one of the most popular sports in the United States. Discover facts about the NFL's biggest winners, record-setting players, and more in this fun, captivating book"— Provided by publisher.
Identifiers: LCCN 2023009266 (print) | LCCN 2023009267 (ebook) | ISBN 9798765608999 (library binding) | ISBN 9798765618820 (epub)
Subjects: LCSH: Football—Miscellanea—Juvenile literature. | BISAC: JUVENILE NONFICTION / Sports & Recreation / Football
Classification: LCC GV950.7 .D627 2024 (print) | LCC GV950.7 (ebook) | DDC 796.332—dc23/eng/20230306

LC record available at https://lccn.loc.gov/2023009266
LC ebook record available at https://lccn.loc.gov/2023009267

ISBN 979-8-7656-2512-5 (pbk.)

Manufactured in the United States of America
1-1009515-51577-5/17/2023

Table of Contents

• • • • • • • • • •

FROM THE BEGINNING

1891 Rutgers University football team

Football started in the mid-1800s.

It was a blend of soccer and rugby.

The National Football League
(NFL) began in 1920.

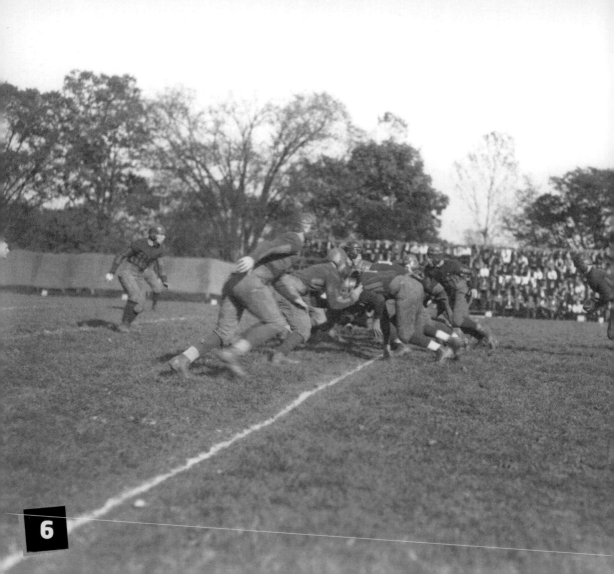

WORLDS CHAMPS
Akron 1920 Professionals

The Akron Pros were the league's first champion.

In 1970, Patricia Palinkas became the first woman to play pro football.

She was a placeholder for the minor-league Orlando Panthers.

Up Next!

RECORD SETTERS.

FANTASTIC FEATS

In 2021, Baltimore Ravens kicker Justin Tucker kicked the longest field goal in NFL history.

It went 66 yards!

Quarterback Tom Brady has the most Super Bowl wins.

He appeared in 10 Super Bowls and won seven of them.

George Blanda played 26 seasons of pro football.

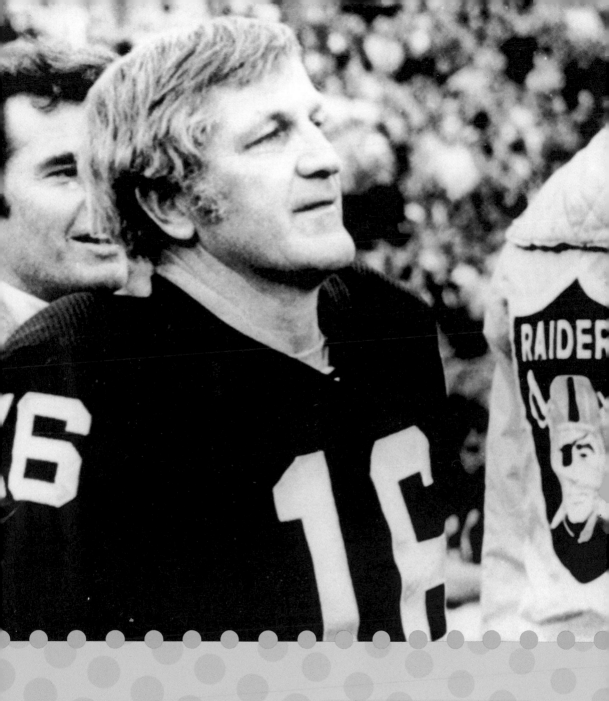

He retired in 1976.

LIST BREAK!

Touchdowns! Who has the most in NFL history?

Passing touchdowns

1.	Tom Brady	649
2.	Drew Brees	571
3.	Peyton Manning	539
4.	Brett Favre	508
5.	Aaron Rodgers	475

Peyton Manning

Stats are accurate through the 2022 NFL season.

Jerry Rice

Receiving touchdowns

1. Jerry Rice   197
2. Randy Moss   156
3. Terrell Owens   153
4. Cris Carter   130
5. Marvin Harrison   128

Up Next!

TEAMWORK.

TEAMING UP

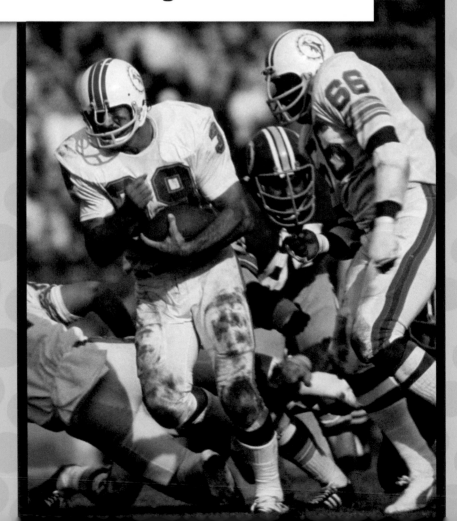

Only one NFL team has ever gone undefeated. In 1972, the Miami Dolphins went 14–0 in the regular season.

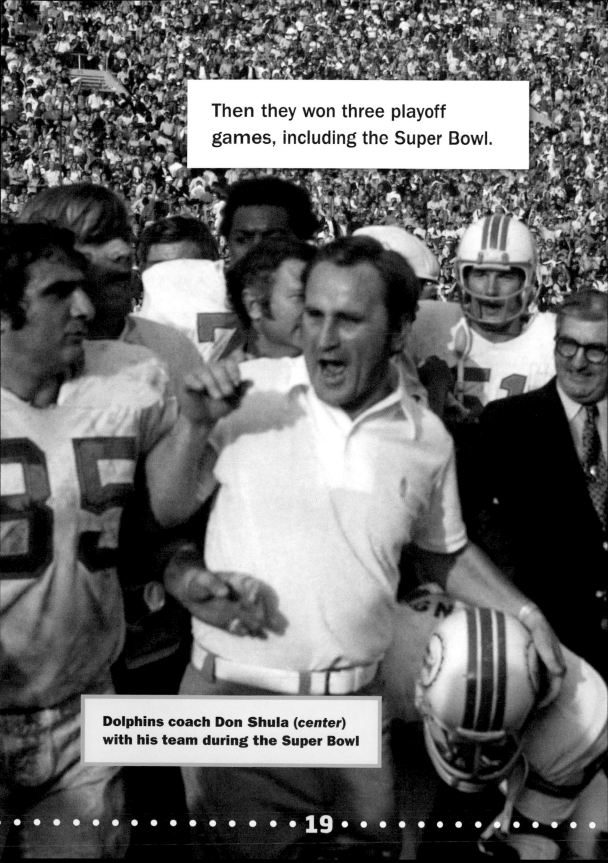

Then they won three playoff games, including the Super Bowl.

Dolphins coach Don Shula (*center*) with his team during the Super Bowl

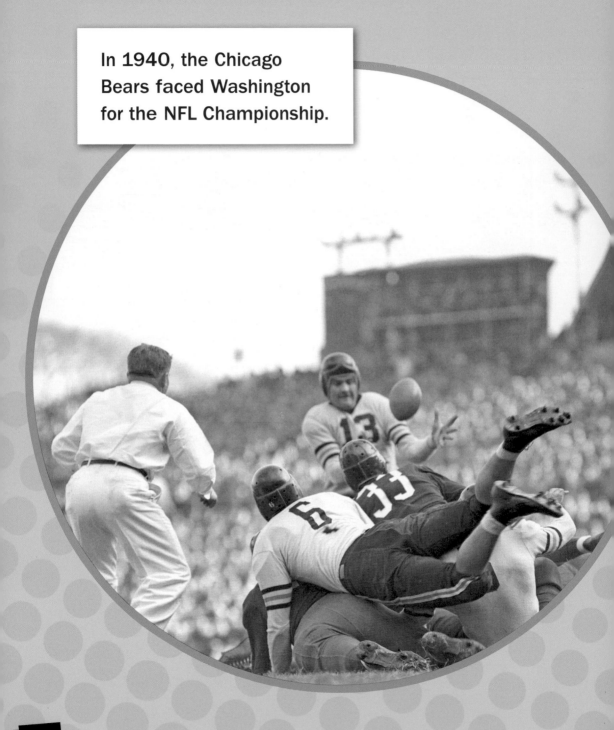

In 1940, the Chicago Bears faced Washington for the NFL Championship.

The Bears won 73–0. It was the biggest score difference in an NFL game.

The Minnesota Vikings had the biggest comeback in NFL history.

In 2022, they trailed the Indianapolis Colts 33–0 at halftime. But the Vikings came back and won 39–36.

Up Next!

UNBELIEVABLE.

AMAZING BUT TRUE

In 1967, the Dallas Cowboys and Green Bay Packers played the Ice Bowl.

It was -13°F (-25°C) during the game.

The New England Patriots played the New York Jets in 2012.

The Patriots scored three touchdowns in 52 seconds.

In 1943, Sammy Baugh threw four touchdown passes and intercepted four passes.

Sammy Baugh

He's the only NFL player to do both in the same game!

Glossary

field goal: a kick worth three points

intercept: when a defender catches a pass intended for a player on the other team

placeholder: the player who holds the ball for the kicker

rugby: a team sport in which players kick, carry, and throw an oval ball

undefeated: having no losses all season

Check It Out!

Downs, Kieran. *Football*. Minneapolis: Bellwether Media, 2024.

Ducksters: Football
https://www.ducksters.com/sports/football.php

Lowe, Alexander. *G.O.A.T. Football Running Backs*. Minneapolis: Lerner Publications, 2023.

National Football League
https://nfl.com

Sports Illustrated Kids: Football
https://www.sikids.com/football

Stabler, David. *Tom Brady vs. Joe Montana: Who Would Win?* Minneapolis: Lerner Publications, 2024.

Index

Photo Acknowledgements

Image credits: kledge/Getty Images, p. 3; FJ Higgins/Underwood Archives/ Getty Images, p. 4; H. Armstrong Roberts/ClassicStock/Getty Images, p. 5; History and Art Collection/Alamy, p. 6; Bruce Bennett Studios/Getty Images Studios/Getty Images, p. 7; Winslow Productions/Getty Images, p. 8; Rick Stewart/Getty Images, p. 9; AP Photo/Duane Burleson, p. 10; AP Photo/Tony Ding, p. 11; Cliff Welch/Icon Sportswire/Getty Images, p. 12; Patrick Smith/Getty Images, p. 13; Focus on Sport/Getty Images, pp. 14, 17, 18, 19; Archive Photos/Getty Images, p. 15; Ronald Martinez/ Getty Images, p. 16; Bettmann/Getty Images, pp. 20, 21, 28, 29; Stephen Maturen/Getty Images, pp. 22, 23; Bruce Bennett Studios/Getty Images Studios/Getty Images, p. 24; AP Photo/File, p. 25; Jim McIsaac/Getty Images, p. 26; Rich Schultz /Getty Images, p. 27.

Cover: AP Photo/Scott Boehm.